My World &GLOBE

BY IRA WOLFMAN

WITH ILLUSTRATIONS BY PAUL MEISEL

WORKMAN PUBLISHING
NEW YORK

LIBRARY OF CONGRESS CATALOGING-IN-PUBLICATION DATA
WOLFMAN, IRA.
MY WORLD & GLOBE (REVISED EDITION) / BY IRA WOLFMAN.
P.   CM.
SUMMARY: INTRODUCES THE GEOGRAPHY OF THE WORLD. INCLUDES AN
INFLATABLE GLOBE ON WHICH BOUNDARIES CAN BE DRAWN, COUNTRIES
LABELED, AND STICKERS
ISBN 0-7611-3069-1 (PBK.)
1. GEOGRAPHY—JUVENILE LITERATURE.   [1. GEOGRAPHY.   2. GLOBES.]
I. TITLE.   II. TITLE: MY WORLD AND GLOBE.
G175.W65 1991
910—DC20   91-50382 CIP AC

THANKS TO EUGENE HARRISON, AT UCLA SCHOOL OF MEDICINE,
PH.D. IN GEOGRAPHY, FOR REVIEWING THE MANUSCRIPT.
THANKS ALSO TO PAUL HANSON, PAUL MEISEL,
MARY WILKINSON, AND ANNE KOSTICK.

DEDICATED WITH LOVE TO RONDA, EVAN, AND PERRY
WHO MEAN THE WORLD TO ME.

CONCEPT AND DESIGN BY PAUL HANSON

WORKMAN BOOKS ARE AVAILABLE AT SPECIAL
DISCOUNTS WHEN PURCHASED IN BULK FOR
PREMIUMS AND SALES PROMOTIONS AS WELL AS
FOR FUND-RAISING OR EDUCATIONAL USE. SPECIAL
EDITIONS OR BOOK EXCERPTS CAN ALSO BE
CREATED TO SPECIFICATION. FOR DETAILS, CONTACT
THE SPECIAL SALES DIRECTOR AT THE ADDRESS BELOW.

WORKMAN PUBLISHING COMPANY
708 BROADWAY
NEW YORK, NY 10003-9555

PRINTED IN CHINA
FIRST PRINTING JULY 2003
10 9 8 7 6 5 4 3 2 1

CONTENTS

CHAPTER ONE

WHERE ARE YOU?

You Can Be in Many Places at the Same Time

Where are you? You may think you know the answer to that question.
"I'm in my room at home."
"I'm at my desk at school."
"I'm in the library."
"I'm on the couch in the living room."
"I'm sitting at the kitchen table."

One of those answers might be right, but it wouldn't be the complete answer. You are in a lot of places—all at the same time.

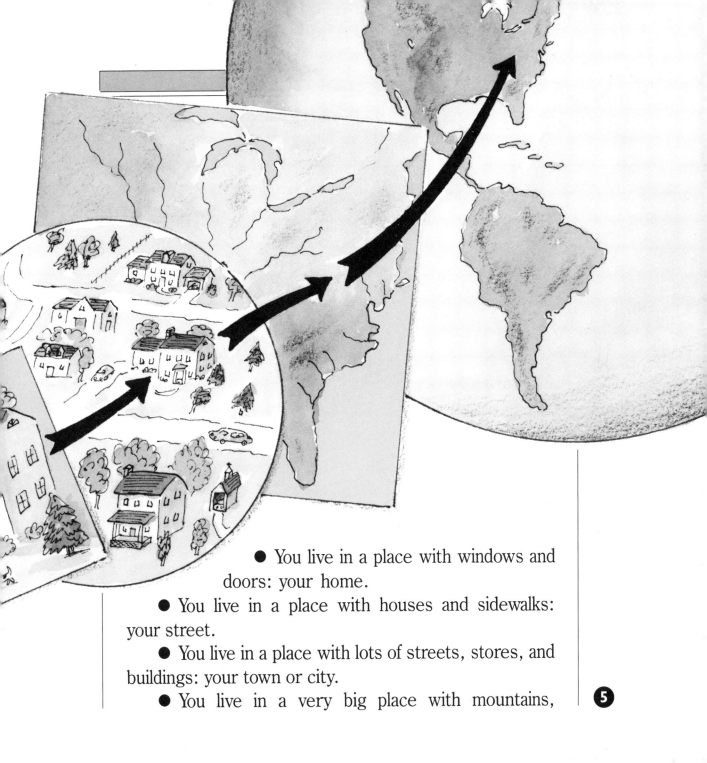

- You live in a place with windows and doors: your home.
- You live in a place with houses and sidewalks: your street.
- You live in a place with lots of streets, stores, and buildings: your town or city.
- You live in a very big place with mountains,

The Big Blue Ball

To see what the whole world really looks like, blow up your globe (you may need some adult help to fill it up completely). As you read this book and learn about geography, you can:

• attach the enclosed stickers (each chapter will help you find the right place for the stickers);

• draw directly on the globe with crayon or washable marker pens—trace travel routes, add borders, spotlight special places;

• add any other stickers or special pictures you may have that will make your globe more interesting.

To hang up your globe, run a string through the loop on the valve.

6

forests, rivers, and valleys: a country called the United States.

● And you live in a place with jungles, deserts, oceans and continents: the planet Earth.

Some of these places—like your street—you can see if you look out a window. Some of them—like your neighborhood or city—you can walk around in.

Other places are so big, you can't see them unless you are up in an airplane or a rocketship.

The Whole World

To get to know all the different places, both big and small, people can study **GEOGRAPHY**.

Geography shows us where these places are and what they're like. Geography helps to explain how people and animals live differently in different places and may also explain how

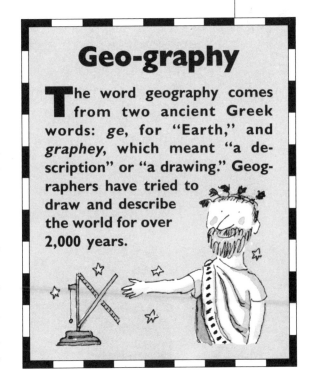

Geo-graphy

The word geography comes from two ancient Greek words: *ge*, for "Earth," and *graphey*, which meant "a description" or "a drawing." Geographers have tried to draw and describe the world for over 2,000 years.

places came to get their names. (Does your town have a name like Clear Lake, Valley Stream, or Boulder? There's probably a reason why!)

Geography can help you understand just where you are. If you know your neighborhood, you can probably find your way to your friend's house, your school, or the park.

Knowing where you are in the world is helpful, too. Do you want to go to a far-away place? Geography can help you find the spot, and figure out the easiest way to get there.

Even if someday you travel out of this world, you'll need to know geography. If a creature on the planet Pluto asks you where you're from, you'll just say, "Earth—the third planet from the sun."

Sticker Tricks

Everyone has a home somewhere on Earth. Ask a parent or older friend to help you find your home on your globe. Attach the **I LIVE HERE** sticker so it points to your home. (Since our world is so big, you won't be able to see the exact spot, but you'll begin to know where in the world you are.)

I LIVE HER

CHAPTER TWO

YOUR SMALL WORLD:
Exploring Your Home and Neighborhood

Explorers are people who travel to new and unknown places. They search for interesting and unusual things, and they try to share what they've found so that everyone can better understand our world.

You are a kind of explorer.

At first you didn't know anything about the world. But as you grew older, you began to learn about it. Now you know the street you live on. You know where some of your friends live, and which store sells ice cream.

You've gone to unfamiliar places and remembered them. You may notice if something in a new place is different or unusual.

Using Geography

So in fact, you already know some geography—the geography of your small world. Here's an example:

Let's say one day you're sitting on your bed, and your mother comes in and asks you to put on your play clothes. You jump up, go to the right side of your room, and open the second drawer of your dresser where the play clothes are.

Without being aware of it, you were using what you know about the "geography" of your room. You know where the dresser is. You know that the play clothes are in the second drawer. And you know exactly how to get there without getting lost.

What a Spider Sees

Close your eyes and imagine your room. Your mind probably makes a picture just like the one you'd see if your eyes were open. But how would the room look to you if you were a spider on the ceiling? Perhaps something like this:

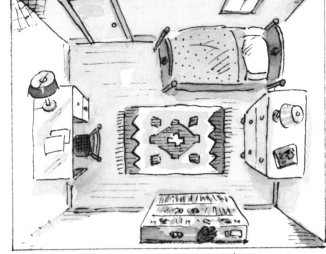

From here it's easy to see the room's "geography"—that is, where things are. This kind of picture is a lot like a map because it tells you many things—the best way to get from your bed to the dresser, for example.

Many of these pictures put together might give you a giant picture, or plan, of your home, showing which rooms are next to which, how big each room is, what shape it is, and what objects are in it.

Outside and Around

Your **NEIGHBORHOOD** is the area around your home. It's the places where you like to go, the streets you always walk on.

What do you know about your neighborhood? You probably know where many things are—like the mailbox, the school, the drug store, the church. You know where the traffic lights are. You know where your playground is, and how long a walk it is to get there. You may know the fastest way to get to your friend's house.

So you've already learned some of the most important geographical features of your neighborhood. You

12

know **LOCATIONS**, like your home address. You also know some **LANDMARKS**— familiar, unusual, or special things that can help you remember where you are.

That's pretty good explorer work!

My Room

X

Draw Your Small World

Pretend you're a spider on the ceiling and draw your room.

Let shapes stand for the furniture and other things in the room (a circle for a table, or a square for a chair, for example).

Color in your picture. Put in an "X" to mark the spot where you are.

Now draw your street (you may have to go outside to draw this picture). Draw only one street or part of the neighborhood. Show where your house is.

What other landmarks can you put in? Add the name of the street. Remember to draw this picture as if you saw it from up high. Mark your spot with an "X."

X

Park

My Street

Church

Market

CHAPTER THREE

MAPS AND GLOBES: Making Pictures of Your World

A map is a lot like the pictures you just drew, but it's a special kind of picture. A map gives information—facts—about a place. There are many kinds of maps that show different kinds of information, but most maps will tell you where a place is, the name of the place, and its size.

The Tale of Scale

Even though some maps are very large, no one needs a map as large as the real place it shows. To be useful, maps have to be much smaller than the places they are showing.

Snapshot

Map

Maps often look something like a picture taken from an airplane. Things seem smaller as you get farther away from them. As an airplane flies higher, some things on the ground get so small that they can no longer be seen. In the same way, the bigger the area a map covers, the fewer small things the map can show.

In order to show things as they really are, a map must be "in scale"—that is, things should seem the right size when compared to other things near them.

A boy and a cat in scale.

A boy and a cat not in scale!

Every Which Way (Or, What SNEW?)

Do you know SNEW? If you do, you'll never be lost, because SNEW stands for:

South, **N**orth, **E**ast, and **W**est.

No matter where you are on Earth, there's only one direction to go to find the North Pole. When you face that way, you're facing north. The same is true for the South Pole.

If you face the sun when it comes up in the morning, you're facing east. And when you watch a beautiful sunset, you're looking to the west.

A compass is a helpful tool when you want to find directions. It has a needle that always points north. If you point your face the same way, your left arm will point west, your right arm will point east, and your back will be to the south.

Map Talk

On a map, a river looks like a wiggly line. A huge city may look like a big dot. That's because maps use a code, made of symbols or of pictures, to give information. To find out what a map's code is, look for the **KEY**— the box that tells you what each symbol means.

KEY	
○	CITY
☆	CAPITAL CITY
～	RIVER
▬	RAILROAD
╱	HIGHWAY
🌲	FOREST
🌵	DESERT
- - -	BOUNDARY LINE
✈	AIRPORT

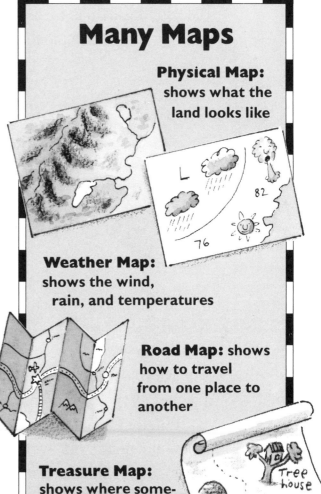

Many Maps

Physical Map: shows what the land looks like

Weather Map: shows the wind, rain, and temperatures

Road Map: shows how to travel from one place to another

Treasure Map: shows where something is hidden!

Round and Round

Maps are flat pictures. But our world is round. How can a map maker put a round picture on a flat map? Think of the round Earth as an orange. You can peel the orange in one piece and flatten it out on a table, but you'd have to stretch some areas and shrink others to make everything fit.

A globe is a better way to show our world as it really is. On a globe, all the continents are the right shapes and sizes.

Whether you're standing in a cornfield or on a mountain peak, our world looks flat. But long before astronauts could see Earth from space, people knew our planet was round. How did they know?

They watched big sailing ships as they sailed out to sea. The ships sailed far away to the **HORIZON** (where the sky meets the sea), and disappeared. First, the ship's bottom disappeared. Next, the mast. Finally, even the top of the sails disappeared.

This proved that Earth must be round! If our planet were flat, the entire ship would simply appear to grow smaller and smaller as it sailed farther away, until it could not be seen.

It's Really Round!

You can see for yourself what scientists of long ago discovered. Put your globe on your lap. Take an object (a crayon, a photograph, or a tall toy) and stand it up in the middle of your globe. Now slowly move it in a straight line away from you, keeping one end of the object on the globe. As you do, you'll see the object slowly disappear—first the bottom, then the middle, then the top.

Where in the World?

If someone asks where you live, you may tell them your street address. But most places on Earth don't have streets. How can you find a spot in the middle of the ocean, or on top of a mountain?

Earth's **axis** is an invisible line that runs right through its center, from north to south.

Invisible Lines

Our world is full of strange lines—but you won't find them painted on the ground. These invisible lines are only on maps and globes, and they help us understand how the world works.

O° Long.

O° Lat.

The **equator** is an invisible line that circles the world around the middle like a belt.

Longitude and **latitude** lines run up and down and across the globe like invisible streets. They're used to find places on Earth.

At each end of the axis is an invisible **pole**.

Map makers invented global "streets" by drawing lines all over the globe. **LONGITUDE** lines run from the North Pole to the South Pole, where they all meet. **LATITUDE** lines circle the globe like belts, running next to each other but never meeting. Every line has a number, called a **DEGREE**, beginning with zero for the **EQUATOR** and also for the **PRIME MERIDIAN**, the longitude line that runs through a town called Greenwich, England.

With latitude and longitude lines, even a tiny island in the ocean can have its own address.

Sticker Tricks

Place these stickers on your globe:

on top of the globe, near the air valve

NORTH POLE

SOUTH POLE

on the bottom of the globe, in the middle of Antarctica

AMAZON RIVER ➡

pointing to the big river in South America

NILE RIVER ➡

pointing to the big river in Africa

CHAPTER FOUR

A WORLD TOUR:

What's Under Your Feet

It happened for the first time in 1961: An astronaut rocketed into space, looked out, and saw a beautiful, giant blue ball hanging in the darkness. It was Earth, our world.

But you don't need to be an astronaut to see the world that way. Just pick up your globe.

A Watery World

What do you see? Just as the astronauts did, you see a round ball, mostly blue. The blue color stands for water, and Earth is almost completely covered with water.

OCEANS are gigantic pools of salty water that stretch many thousands of miles around Earth. There are four big oceans on our planet. To find the largest

one, turn the globe until you see a side that is almost all blue. That's the **PACIFIC OCEAN**. The Pacific Ocean is so big, all of the land on our planet could fit into it—with room to spare!

If you turn the globe to the opposite side, you'll find the **ATLANTIC OCEAN**, the second-largest body of water. The next-largest ocean is located near the country of India, and it is called the **INDIAN OCEAN**. The smallest ocean is the **ARCTIC OCEAN**, around the North Pole.

Many smaller bodies of water—seas, lakes, rivers, bays, and gulfs—are scattered around our planet. And there are also giant frozen rivers, called glaciers, in the far northern and far southern areas.

Half a World

Half of a globe is known as a **hemisphere**. The equator divides your globe into a Northern Hemisphere and a Southern Hemisphere. Cutting a globe from the North Pole down along the prime meridian divides it into an Eastern Hemisphere and a Western Hemisphere. Australia is in the Southern Hemisphere, but it is also in the Eastern Hemisphere. Where are the other continents?

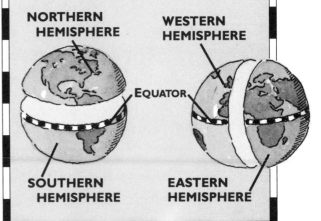

NORTHERN HEMISPHERE

WESTERN HEMISPHERE

EQUATOR

SOUTHERN HEMISPHERE

EASTERN HEMISPHERE

Looking at the Land

Brown is the color of land as astronauts see it from space. (On your globe, the land is green.) The land on which we live is made up mostly of rock, soil, and sand. There are many different kinds of land—high and low places, flat and bumpy places, and wet and dry places.

The world's land is divided into seven giant pieces called **CONTINENTS**. Millions of people live on six of these continents. The seventh, **ANTARCTICA**, is much too cold for humans to live there easily; it is home to penguins and to a few scientists studying this cold continent.

MOUNTAINS are the tallest places on the continents, rising high above the land around them. Mountains are often found in groups called **MOUNTAIN CHAINS**. You can see a few of these mountain chains on

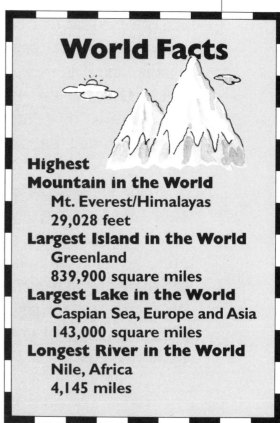

World Facts

Highest Mountain in the World
Mt. Everest/Himalayas
29,028 feet

Largest Island in the World
Greenland
839,900 square miles

Largest Lake in the World
Caspian Sea, Europe and Asia
143,000 square miles

Longest River in the World
Nile, Africa
4,145 miles

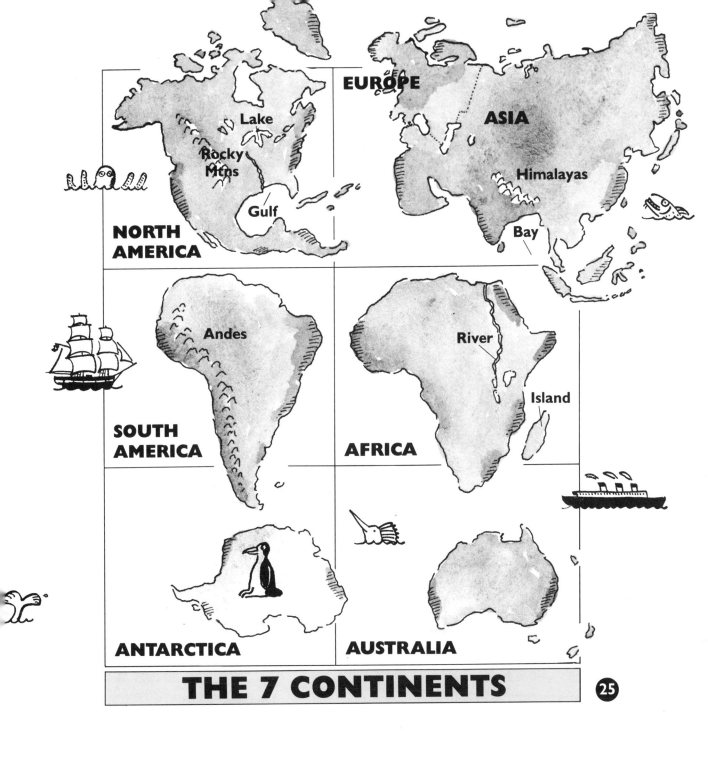

EUROPE

ASIA

Lake

Himalayas

Rocky
Mtns

Gulf

Bay

**NORTH
AMERICA**

Andes

River

Island

**SOUTH
AMERICA**

AFRICA

ANTARCTICA

AUSTRALIA

THE 7 CONTINENTS

your globe. The **ROCKY MOUNTAINS** are located not far from the Pacific Ocean, on the continent of North America.

The **ANDES** stand in a line along the edge of South America, near the Pacific Ocean.

The tallest mountain chain in the world is called the **HIMALAYAS**. These huge mountains are in Asia, not far from the Indian Ocean.

FLATLANDS are the places where most people live. In flat places, it's easier for people to grow food, build houses, travel, and work. There are many kinds of flatlands:

DESERTS:
hot, dry

TUNDRAS:
cold, often frozen

PLAINS: grassy,
warm or hot

FORESTS:
filled with trees

Smaller land forms known as **ISLANDS** can be found all over the globe. Sometimes islands form long chains in the middle of the ocean.

The state of Hawaii is actually a group of islands in the Pacific Ocean.

VALLEYS: low areas between hills or mountains

RAINFORESTS: hot, wet

Sticker Tricks

Place these stickers on your globe:

in the Himalayas

MT. EVEREST

PENGUIN

on the continent of Antarctica

on the continent of Africa, near the prime meridian

DESERT

HAWAII

on the small island chain in the Pacific Ocean between North America and Asia

CHAPTER FIVE

SPACESHIP EARTH:
A New Journey Each Day and Year

Sit very still for a minute. Do you feel anything moving? Even if you can't feel it, you are on a kind of giant spaceship. The spaceship is our planet Earth, and it's been traveling through space for billions of years. Earth travels in two *different* ways.

The Way We Get Day

First, our world spins on its axis like a top. To see how, put one hand on your globe's North Pole, and the other hand on the South Pole. Now spin your globe slowly from left to right:

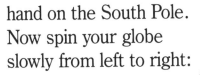

Your globe is turning, or **ROTATING**, just as Earth does. This rotating motion, along with the light from the sun, causes night and day. When sunlight shines on a part of Earth, it is daytime there. But only half of Earth can face the sun at any time. In the part of Earth facing away from the sun, there is no light and it is nighttime.

But since our planet is always rotating, the place where it is now day will face away from the sun in a few hours, and then it will become night. And the place where it is now dark will then be bright and full of daylight.

It takes Earth 24 hours to spin completely around one time. That's why each day is 24 hours long.

29

Night and Day

You can create night and day on your globe with a flashlight and a friend.

Try this in a darkened room. Have your friend hold the globe with the continent you live on facing toward you. Stand a few feet away and shine your flashlight directly at the equator. It's now midday in your part of the world. In what part of the world is it the middle of the night?

Ask your friend to turn the globe slowly from left to right. Stop when the sun is setting over your home. In what part of the world is the sun rising?

Time After Time

When it's the middle of the night in Los Angeles, California, it is morning in London, England. But what *time* is it in each of those places?

To help people keep track of time, the world was divided into 24 **TIME ZONES**. In each zone, the time is one hour different from the zone next to it. If you cross one time zone going east, you have to turn your watch ahead one hour; 9 o'clock becomes 10 o'clock. If you cross a time zone going west, you turn your watch back one hour; 9 o'clock becomes 8 o'clock.

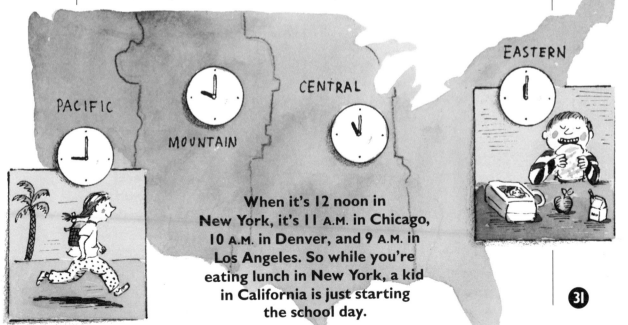

EASTERN

CENTRAL

PACIFIC

MOUNTAIN

When it's 12 noon in New York, it's 11 A.M. in Chicago, 10 A.M. in Denver, and 9 A.M. in Los Angeles. So while you're eating lunch in New York, a kid in California is just starting the school day.

Yesterday or Tomorrow?

All 24 time zones put together equal 24 hours—the same as a day. If you traveled all the way around the world, you'd gain or lose a day! Scientists agreed on one line, the International Date Line, that would divide one day from another.

Earth Facts

- Earth is not perfectly round. It is a little wider at the equator, and it's a little flattened at the North and South Poles.
- The equator is 24,902 miles long. You'd need more than 40 million men's belts to put a belt around Earth's middle!
- Earth spins at a speed of more than 1,000 miles per hour.

Step across this line going east and today turns into yesterday!

2 MONDAY

1 SUNDAY

One Trip a Year

Planet Earth isn't just rotating. It is also moving in a giant circle, or **REVOLVING**, around the sun. It takes 365 days for Earth to make one complete trip around the sun. That's why 365 days make one year. Our trip looks like this:

Round Trips

How many trips around the sun has Earth made since you were born? It's easy to figure out. Your birthday is the day that Earth is back at the same place it was on the day you were born. If you are four years old, you've been on four complete trips around the sun. If you're five, five trips. How many trips around the sun have your parents made?

The Earth Goes Tilt!

Some people live where it is always hot. Others live where it is always cold. But most people live where the weather changes every few months. These changes are called SEASONS. Earth has four seasons: spring, summer, autumn, and winter.

We have seasons because our world is tilted. In July the Northern Hemisphere is leaning *toward* the sun.

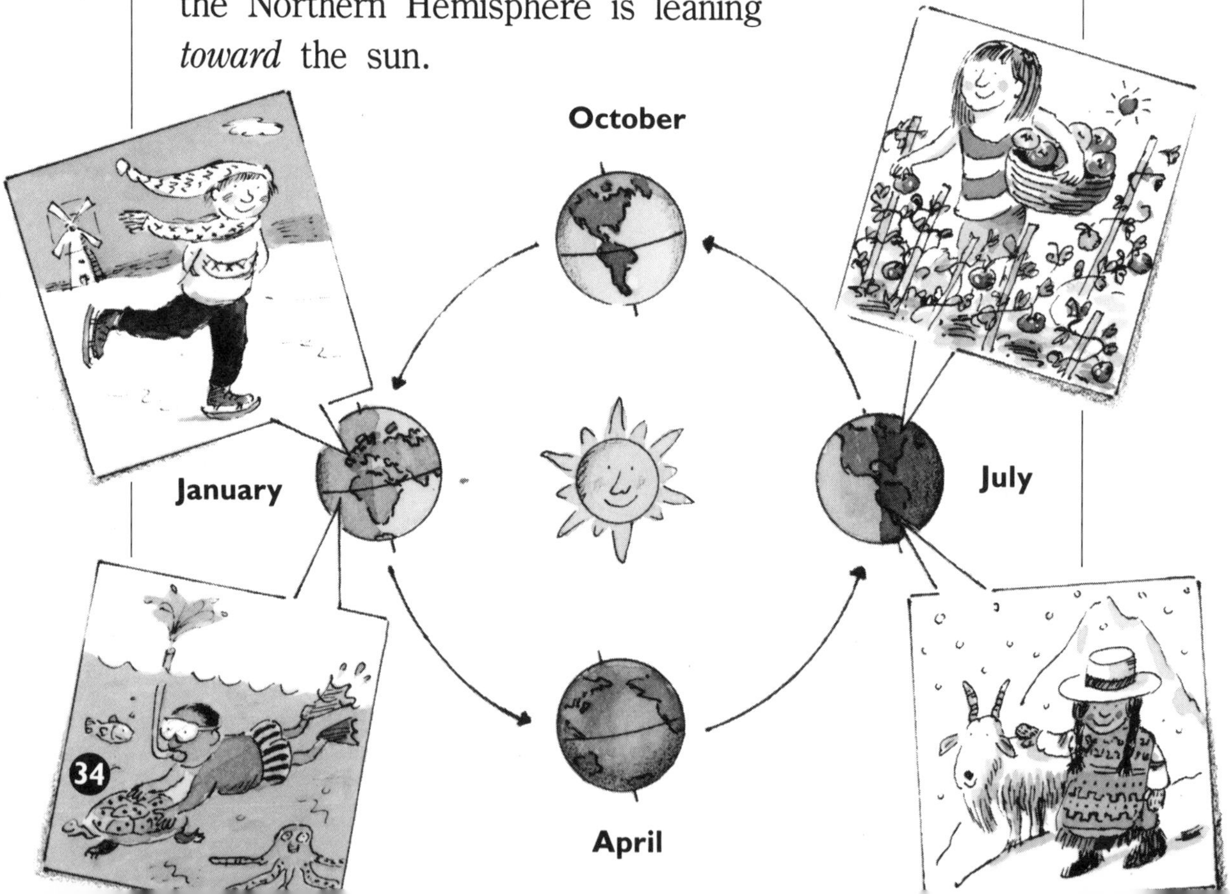

October

January

July

April

34

That makes it a hot time of year, called summer. At the same time, the Southern Hemisphere is leaning *away* from the sun, and it is colder there. So in July, it's winter in the Southern Hemisphere!

A few months later, as the world circles around the sun, the Northern Hemisphere leans away from it, but the Southern Hemisphere leans toward it. That's why the month of January is summertime in South America and Australia, and wintertime in North America and Europe.

At the equator, the sunlight is very strong and it is hot all year. And at the North and South Poles, the sun's light is weaker and the climate is always cold.

Sticker Tricks

Place these stickers on your globe:

Put the current season on your Hemisphere (Northern or Southern).

Put the opposite season on the opposite Hemisphere.

Put the DAY sticker on your Hemisphere (Eastern or Western).

Put the NIGHT sticker on the opposite Hemisphere.

SUMMER

AUTUMN

WINTER

SPRING

DAY

NIGHT

CHAPTER SIX

FIRE AND ICE:
The Earth Is Always Changing

Your globe is a smooth ball that is peaceful and quiet. But the real Earth isn't smooth or peaceful. Our planet is rumpled and crinkly. There are holes in its surface and peaks that stretch above it. Huge ridges and valleys are everywhere, even under the oceans. Earth has bare, sandy deserts that get almost no water, and thick green forests where it rains every day.

And Earth is not quiet. Wind and water wear down its mountains. The ground shakes and quakes. Rivers rush by rocks, and water breaks those rocks into pebbles. Slowly, the face of our world changes.

Most of these changes take a very long time. But they are happening, little by little, every day.

If all of Earth's water and ice could be removed, the planet would look like this

Continents on the Move

Take a look at the continents of South America and Africa. Do they look like pieces of a jigsaw puzzle?

Alfred Wegener, a scientist looking at a globe a hundred years ago, thought so. He measured all the other continents and found that North America could fit into the coastlines of North Africa, Europe, and Greenland.

"Could all the continents have ever been joined together—and then moved apart?" he wondered.

Later, Wegener learned something that convinced him he must be right. The same kinds of dinosaur bones were found in both North America and Europe. The dinosaurs couldn't have swum across the Atlantic Ocean—and they surely didn't take a ship! But if, long ago when dinosaurs were alive, the continents were connected, they might have *walked* across the land. Then, slowly, over millions of years, the continents split and drifted apart.

When Wegener announced his theory, many people didn't believe him. Today, most scientists not only agree with him, they have found that the continents are still slowly drifting apart. They call that supercontinent by the name he invented: *Pangaea*, which means "all lands."

What's Inside?

People can see only one part of Earth. We all live on the outside part, a thin skin called the **CRUST**. The crust is broken into pieces called **PLATES**. The continents are the parts of plates that rise above the oceans. The plates float on top of the **MANTLE**, which is made of hot melted rock called **MAGMA**. The center of Earth is called the **CORE**.

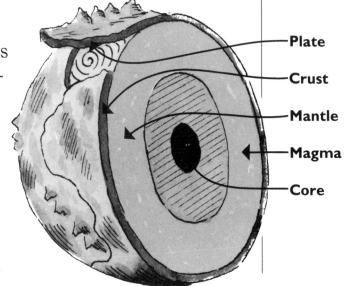

- Plate
- Crust
- Mantle
- Magma
- Core

38

Mountains Going Up!

Mountains rise far above the land around them. Next to some mountains, a skyscraper looks tiny. For example, the Sears Tower in Chicago is the tallest building in America. But you'd have to pile 20 Sears Towers, one on top of the other, to get up to the peak of Mount Everest, the tallest mountain on Earth.

Scientists think that most mountains were created by gigantic collisions. Parts of our world's crust smashed together, and plates slid under one another. Gradually, the top plates were squeezed and pushed up. Mount Everest and the Himalayas were created when the land that today is India slammed into Asia.

Colossal Collisions

Take two thin paper plates and place them about four inches apart on a tabletop. Slowly move one toward the other, sliding one plate gently under the other. Notice how the top plate shows almost no sign of what's going on under it.

Now try it again, moving the plates so they meet just at the edges. Slowly push one edge against the other. Does one plate push its way over the other? Do the plates push up together? Does one plate "flip" the edge of the other? Imagine this happening to a whole continent!

Cones of Fire

A volcano is a kind of tunnel to the center of Earth. Most volcanoes are quiet for a long time. But once in a while, the magma from deep inside Earth shoots up through the tunnel in an explosion of red-hot rock called LAVA. Undersea volcanoes create new islands when cooled lava builds up high enough to rise above the ocean.

Many of Earth's volcanoes can be found where two plates of its crust come together, especially along a big circle around the Pacific Ocean. This circle is called the "Ring of Fire."

Hi, Surtsey! Aloha, Loihi!

In 1963, a new island was born in the sea near Iceland. It was an undersea volcano that had just grown above the ocean's surface. The island was given the name Surtsey. Now that Surtsey has cooled down, plants and birds are beginning to live on it.

Loihi is a volcanic island that has not yet been born. Right now it's an underwater mountain, near the island of Hawaii, growing taller all the time. When will you be able to visit Loihi? Not for about 70,000 years!

This map shows the locations of volcanoes along the "Ring of Fire."

What's Shaking?

The land rumbles and shakes. Buildings sway and fall down. Giant cracks appear in the ground. It's an earthquake!

Earthquakes happen all over the world. When Earth's crust is squeezed, pushed, or pulled too much, it may move suddenly. Like volcanoes, most earthquakes happen near places where two plates come together.

Deep Freeze

In parts of the world it is white and frozen all year long.

The North Pole is in the part of the Arctic Ocean that is always solid ice because it is so cold. The South Pole is on land—the continent of Antarctica—that is frozen and covered with deep layers of snow and ice that never melt.

Millions of years ago, the world was much colder, and the ice and snow of the polar caps covered more of the land. The oceans were smaller because more of the world's water was frozen. Then, as the world slowly became warmer, the ice melted.

GLACIERS are giant rivers of ice that move very slowly down from the coldest places—polar areas or high mountain tops. Glaciers move very slowly, but as they move they carve out

Temperature Facts

The Hottest Day in the Hottest Place on Earth

On September 13, 1922, in Al-Aziziyah, Libya, it was 136 degrees Fahrenheit *above zero.*

The Coldest Day in the Coldest Place on Earth

On July 21, 1983, in Vostok, Antarctica, it was 128.6 degrees Fahrenheit *below zero.*

valleys and make new rivers, hills, and lakes. Even though the world is much warmer today than it was long ago, there are still moving glaciers. You can see them in Alaska, Canada, Greenland, and the Swiss Alps.

Sticker Tricks

Place these stickers on your globe:

on the west coast of Africa

MOVING PLATE ➡

on the east coast of South America

⬅ MOVING PLATE

in Alaska

GLACIER

VOLCANO

on the Ring of Fire

43

CHAPTER SEVEN

ANIMAL ATTRACTIONS:
How They Live and Where to Find Them

There are millions of different creatures living on Earth. You probably have seen animals from faraway places in a zoo, but do you know where they come from?

Every kind of animal has special needs for food and a comfortable home. Some kinds of animals can live in many places, especially if the **CLIMATE** (the year-round weather) is mild—that is, if it's not too hot or too cold, not too wet or too dry—and if there's enough food. Dogs, for example, live in many places in the world.

Over thousands of years, some kinds of animals have changed to make it easier for them to live in harsh climates. In hot, dry climates, there are animals who don't need a lot of water. In cold climates, there are animals who can keep warm easily. That's why the Sahara Desert has its camel and the Arctic Ocean has its walrus.

Some birds travel a long way to stay in their favorite climate all year round. The Arctic tern is the world's greatest animal traveler. It spends summers at the North Pole, then flies to the South Pole to spend summers there, too!

45

World Weather

The climate of a place depends on several things, but mostly on how far it is from the equator. The area above and below the equator is called the **TORRID ZONE**. It is

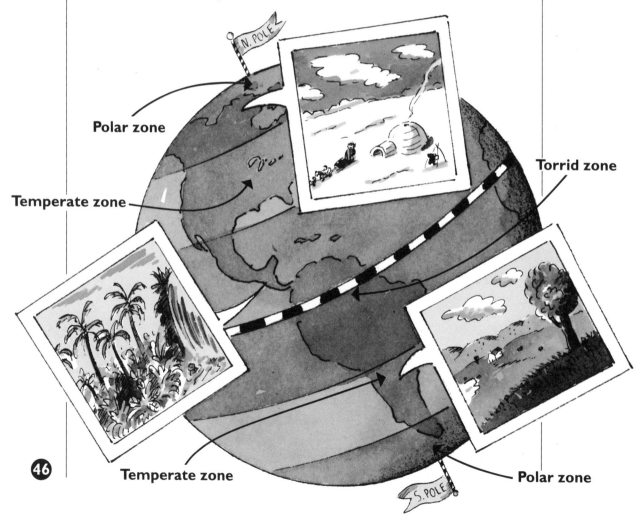

Polar zone

Temperate zone

Torrid zone

Temperate zone

Polar zone

hottest and rainiest in most of the land right on the equator. Most rainforests grow here, and they are home to thousands of kinds of brightly colored tropical plants, fish, birds, and other animals. But some parts of the torrid zone are hot, dry deserts.

The **POLAR ZONES** are wide circles around the North and South Poles. Inside the circles, the weather is cold all year round, and winters are very long. Animals living in polar zones must have thick fur or layers of fat to stay warm.

In between the torrid and polar zones are the **TEMPERATE ZONES**. Here the climate can be hot or cold, wet or dry, depending on ocean currents and whether the land is high or low.

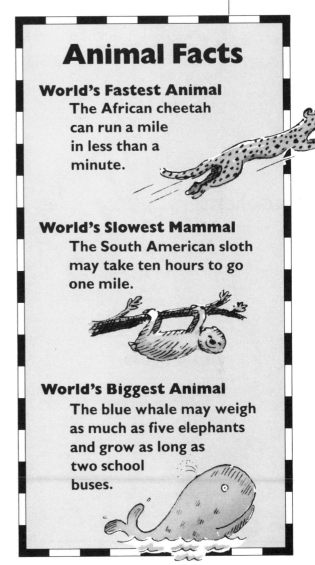

Animal Facts

World's Fastest Animal
The African cheetah can run a mile in less than a minute.

World's Slowest Mammal
The South American sloth may take ten hours to go one mile.

World's Biggest Animal
The blue whale may weigh as much as five elephants and grow as long as two school buses.

Here's where you'll find certain kinds of animals:

FORESTS:
squirrels, bears,
deer, raccoons

GRASSLANDS:
antelope, elephants,
giraffes, lions,
prairie dogs, bison

RAINFORESTS:
monkeys, snakes, apes

MOUNTAINS:
llamas, yaks,
mountain gorillas ,
goats, sheep

DESERTS:
camels,
lizards

OCEANS: octopuses,
dolphins, whales,
fish, sharks

POLAR ZONES:
penguins, walruses,
polar bears, reindeers

48

Strange Faces

Some places have animals that are different from any others on Earth. These places are usually separated by water from other lands.

Australia is far from other continents. There (and nowhere else) you'll find the kangaroo, wallaby, koala, platypus, and black swan.

The Galapagos Islands are tiny islands in the Pacific Ocean off the coast of South America—and the only place where a Galapagos tortoise or a flightless cormorant will live.

Sticker Tricks

Place these stickers on your globe:

in central Africa

in Australia

in northern Africa

in South America, near the equator

KANGAROO

ELEPHANT

CAMEL

TOUCAN

CHAPTER EIGHT

PEOPLE, PLACES, AND THINGS:

How Humans Live in the World

Geography can tell you many things about the world of animals and nature, but it can also tell you about how humans have changed our world over the years, and how we live in it today.

There's almost no place on Earth that people have not at least visited. On most continents people have changed the places where they live, and they keep on changing them. Some changes, such as roads and buildings, can easily be seen. Some, such as separations between states or between countries, can only be shown on maps and globes.

50

Capital Ideas

People have divided the places where they live into **COUNTRIES** (or **NATIONS**), and **CITIES, TOWNS,** or **VILLAGES.** The line between two countries, for example, is called a **BORDER** or **BOUNDARY.** There are over 190 countries in the world. Many maps and globes show different countries by using different colors. They may show borders and boundaries with dotted lines. **CAPITAL CITIES** (the main cities where governments work) are often marked with stars.

Sometimes, the names of countries or their boundary lines change when governments change or when one country takes over another country in war. Then new maps must be made to show the new boundaries and new names. Sometimes, the people of a town or village change its name to something they like better.

WELCOME TO WESTVILLE

WELCOME TO EASTVILLE

Just Around the Corner

Today we know many things about the world, and it doesn't seem so strange or mysterious. But there was a time when the people who lived in the Western Hemisphere knew almost nothing about the people who lived in the Eastern Hemisphere. Wide oceans separated the continents, and people were afraid to cross them.

1492

This map made Columbus think the journey to Asia would be easy. He didn't know there was something missing from the map—North and South America.

One explorer finally proved that the world really *was* round. In 1519, Ferdinand Magellan sailed out of Spain, heading west. Three years later, one of his ships returned from the east. It had traveled all the way around the world.

1519

52

About 500 years ago, explorers from Europe began looking for a shorter path to the faraway Asian countries of India, China, and Japan. They hoped to find them by sailing west across the Atlantic Ocean.

Christopher Columbus and other explorers commanded big ships on long journeys. But instead of arriving in Asia, they discovered two continents—North and South America—they never knew existed. Because they thought they were in India, the explorers called the American people "Indians."

The meeting of these peoples changed world history. Other explorers and then many settlers began coming to these lands, which are still sometimes called the "New World."

Great Circles

Measure travel routes using your globe and a piece of string. Tie a knot at one end of the string. Place the knot over New York City, and stretch the string across the United States and the Pacific Ocean to Tokyo, Japan. Mark the string where it crosses over Tokyo. Now stretch the same string from New York City to Tokyo, but let it cross the Arctic Ocean near the North Pole. Is the distance between the two cities longer or shorter when traveled over the North Pole? This path is called a **GREAT CIRCLE ROUTE**. On a flat map, the distance between New York and Tokyo seems much greater than it really is.

Dug-Up Shortcuts

Ships traveling from the Atlantic Ocean to the Pacific Ocean may sail through a 40-mile-long ditch filled with water—the Panama Canal. Until 1914, when people finished building the canal, ships had to sail thousands of extra miles, all the way around South America. Canals have been dug all over the world. Egypt's famous Suez Canal connects the Mediterranean Sea and the Red Sea.

Where Does It All Come From?

Did you ever eat a pineapple or a banana? Play a game with a rubber ball? Watch someone put gasoline into a car? All those things probably come from somewhere very far from your home.

Pineapples, bananas, and rubber come from plants that grow in tropical places like Hawaii and Guatemala.

Gasoline comes from oil, and oil is found in only a few places on Earth. The gas in your family car may have come from the American states of Texas, Louisiana, or Alaska, or it might have come from a country like Saudi Arabia or Indonesia.

Your favorite things can come from all over the world!

Baseball bat from United States

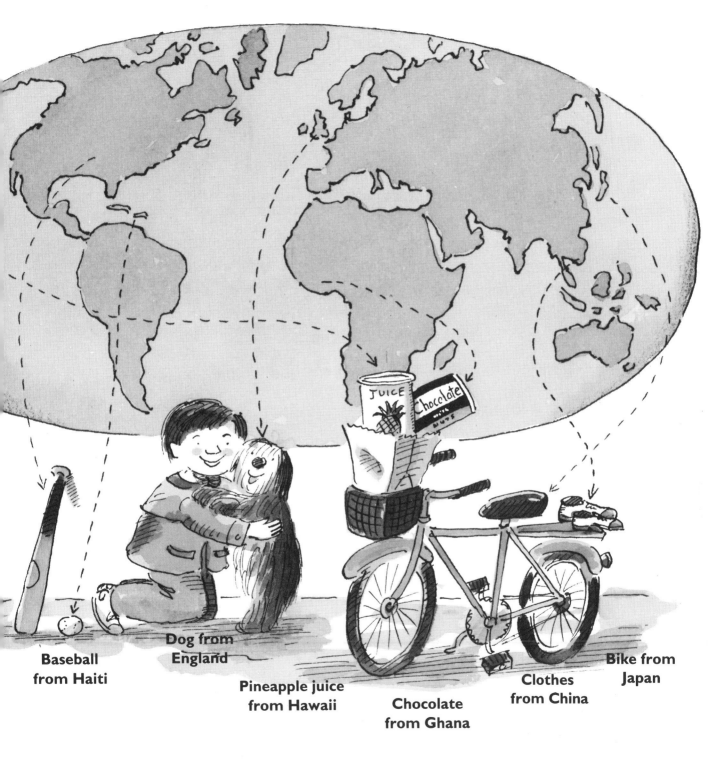

Baseball from Haiti

Dog from England

Pineapple juice from Hawaii

Chocolate from Ghana

Clothes from China

Bike from Japan

Many places in the world grow or make something special. Some of the rice we eat comes from China and other countries in Asia. Tea leaves may come from India, and coffee beans may come from South America or Africa.

Some cars are built in the United States. Other cars are built in Japan, Sweden, and Germany. Your shoes or pants may have been made in China or Mexico.

How Does It All Get Here?

If you want to eat a banana, you don't have to travel to Guatemala, where bananas grow. Just go down to the corner grocery store. And if your mom wants to fill up the family car, she can go to a nearby gas station.

The bananas, the gasoline, and many other things you use every day traveled across the world to get to you. When people who want things pay money or

56

goods to the people who have them, the exchange is called **TRADE**.

For thousands of years, people have been trading things from faraway places. Spices like cinnamon and cloves were loaded on sailing ships. The ships spent months crossing the ocean. Today, products travel long distances very quickly. Lumber made from trees in the state of Oregon is put on a train or a truck and sent to Texas. Beautiful jewelry made in Africa or Asia is flown to the United States by airplane. These trips may take only a few days. Huge oil tankers bring millions of barrels of oil across the ocean in only a week.

Sticker Tricks

Place these stickers on your globe:

on the islands where he first landed, between North and South America

COLUMBUS

near the Panama Canal

BANANAS

in the Persian Gulf

OIL

at the southern tip of South America

MAGELLAN

CHAPTER NINE

THINKING GLOBALLY: Get to Know Your World

THE TAJ MAHAL
a beautiful white marble memorial building in India

Someday you may become a world traveler. But right now you can explore the world without leaving home by studying maps and globes.

There are more than 6 billion people on Earth, and they are alike in many ways—many of them have families, go to school, and work. But life can be very different from one place to another. People around the world live in many types of houses. Their clothing, food, language, and even the games they play may be different from yours. One way to learn about the many kinds of people on the planet is to look at a special book of maps called an **ATLAS.**

Worldwide Wonders

Almost every place in the world has something special about it. Some countries claim the tallest skyscraper, the oldest church, the most beautiful waterfall, or the longest river. The place may be known only to the people who live in the area, or it may be a world-famous landmark.

Every landmark has a story to tell about how it came to be built or discovered, and about the people who made it or used it.

THE STATUE OF LIBERTY the symbol of freedom that stands on an island in New York Harbor

MACHU PICCHU "Lost City" of the Incas of Peru

STONEHENGE an ancient, mysterious ring of stones in England

Sticker Tricks

Many of the places and landmarks in this chapter can be found on your sticker sheet. Use a map to help you place the stickers on your globe.

THE PYRAMIDS OF EGYPT giant stone tombs of ancient Egyptian kings

THE GREAT WALL OF CHINA a gigantic wall that stretches thousands of miles across China

What Does That Name Mean?

Most names mean something. Puerto Rico, for example, is Spanish for "rich port." Here are some other country and city names and what they mean:

COSTA RICA: rich coast
FLORIDA: the place with flowers
MASSACHUSETTS: the big land
WASHINGTON: named after the first U.S. president

PHOENIX: an ancient bird
TOGO: by the water's edge
AUSTRALIA: the southern lands
LOUISIANA: named after King Louis of France
MANHATTAN: island of rolling hills

Small Talk

There are thousands of different languages in the world, and almost every language has a word that means "hello." Here's how people say hello in some languages other than English:

BUENOS DIAS (Spanish)

BONJOUR (French)

GUTEN TAG (German)

O-HI-O (Japanese)

SALAAM (Arabic)

NEE-HOW (Chinese)

Showing Colors

Every country has a flag—a piece of cloth with a pattern or picture that symbolizes a country, and that sometimes tells a story about its history. You probably are familiar with a few flags—the one for your own country, for example. Learning to recognize the flags of all the countries of the world may take you a while—there are over 190 of them!

Play Geography

Geography can be a game. There are many ways to play it, but try the simple way described below.

Starting with the first letter of the alphabet, name a country, state, or town that begins with each letter, working your way from A to Z. Here's a list to start you off:

A	Africa	**J**	Japan	**S**	Santiago
B	Bombay	**K**	Korea	**T**	Tanzania
C	China	**L**	Liberia	**U**	United States
D	Denmark	**M**	Moscow	**V**	Vietnam
E	England	**N**	New Zealand	**W**	Washington
F	France	**O**	Ohio	**X**	Xai-Xai
G	Greenland	**P**	Puerto Rico	**Y**	Yugoslavia
H	Holland	**Q**	Quebec	**Z**	Zambia
I	Italy	**R**	Rhode Island		

United States

United Kingdom

Israel

Lebanon

Canada

Japan

JAMBO (Swahili)

61

NORTH AND SOUTH AMERICA

1. The Bahamas
2. Cuba
3. Jamaica
4. Haiti
5. Dominican Republic
6. Antigua and Barbuda
7. St. Kitts and Nevis
8. Dominica
9. St. Lucia
10. Barbados
11. St. Vincent and the Grenadines
12. Grenada
13. Trinidad and Tobago
14. Guyana
15. Suriname
16. Canada
17. United States
18. Mexico
19. Belize
20. Guatemala
21. El Salvador
22. Honduras
23. Nicaragua
24. Costa Rica
25. Panama
26. Venezuela
27. Colombia
28. Ecuador
29. Peru
30. Brazil
31. Bolivia
32. Paraguay
33. Uruguay
34. Argentina
35. Chile

EUROPE

36. Iceland
37. United Kingdom
38. Ireland
39. Denmark
40. Germany
41. Netherlands
42. Luxembourg
43. Belgium
44. Finland
45. Sweden
46. Norway
47. Estonia
48. Latvia
49. Lithuania
50. Poland
51. Belarus
52. Romania
53. Moldova
54. Greece
55. Bulgaria
56. Ukraine
57. Turkey
58. Cyprus
59. Czech Republic
60. Slovakia
61. Austria
62. Hungary
63. France
64. Switzerland
65. Spain
66. Portugal
67. Italy
68. Slovenia
69. Croatia
70. Bosnia and Herzegovina
71. Serbia and Montenegro
72. Macedonia
73. Albania
74. Andorra
75. Liechtenstein
76. Malta
77. San Marino
78. Monaco

AFRICA

79. Tunisia
80. Morocco
81. Algeria
82. Libya
83. Egypt
84. Mauritania
85. Cape Verde
86. Senegal
87. The Gambia
88. Guinea-Bissau
89. Mali
90. Guinea
91. Sierra Leone
92. Liberia
93. Ivory Coast
94. Burkina Faso
95. Ghana
96. Togo
97. Benin
98. Niger
99. Nigeria
100. Chad
101. São Tomé and Príncipe
102. Cameroon
103. Equatorial Guinea
104. Gabon
105. Central African Republic
106. Congo
107. Sudan
108. Angola
109. Dem. Republic of the Congo
110. Namibia
111. Botswana
112. Zambia
113. Zimbabwe
114. South Africa
115. Lesotho
116. Swaziland
117. Mozambique
118. Malawi
119. Seychelles
120. Comoros
121. Mauritius
122. Madagascar
123. Uganda
124. Kenya
125. Tanzania
126. Rwanda
127. Burundi
128. Somalia
129. Djibouti
130. Eritrea
131. Ethiopia

ASIA

132. Georgia
133. Armenia
134. Azerbaijan
135. Syria
136. Lebanon
137. Iraq
138. Oman
139. United Arab Emirates
140. Bahrain
141. Qatar
142. Kuwait
143. Saudi Arabia
144. Jordan
145. Israel
146. Yemen
147. Turkmenistan
148. Uzbekistan
149. Tajikistan
150. Kazakhstan
151. Kyrgyzstan
152. Iran
153. Afghanistan
154. Pakistan
155. Sri Lanka
156. Maldives
157. Bhutan
158. Nepal
159. India
160. Bangladesh
161. Myanmar
162. Indonesia
163. East Timor
164. Russia
165. Mongolia
166. China
167. Japan
168. North Korea
169. South Korea
170. Vietnam
171. Laos
172. Thailand
173. Cambodia
174. Philippines
175. Malaysia
176. Brunei
177. Singapore

PACIFIC

178. Australia
179. New Zealand
180. Papua New Guinea
181. Solomon Islands
182. Fiji
183. Nauru
184. Vanuatu
185. Kiribati
186. Samoa
187. Tuvalu
188. Tonga
189. Palau
190. Micronesia
191. Marshall Islands

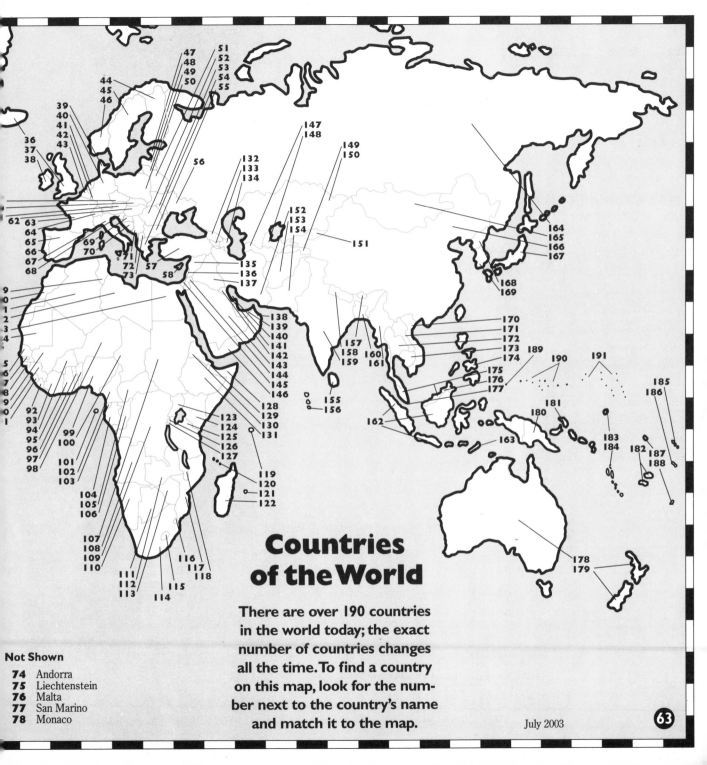

Countries of the World

There are over 190 countries in the world today; the exact number of countries changes all the time. To find a country on this map, look for the number next to the country's name and match it to the map.

Not Shown

74	Andorra
75	Liechtenstein
76	Malta
77	San Marino
78	Monaco

July 2003

Sticker Key

This key will help you place the rest of the stickers on your globe. You may also want to look at the map on the previous page to find countries. If your favorite country or city is not on the sticker sheet, add it using one of the blank stickers.

GREENLAND→ on the large island northeast of North America

MADAGASCAR→ on the island off the east coast of Africa

BEIJING→ capital city of China

TOKYO→ capital city of Japan

PARIS→ capital city of France

MOSCOW→ capital city of Russia

SANTIAGO→ capital city of Chile

BOMBAY→ city on the west coast of India

BUENOS AIRES→ capital city of Argentina

CAPE TOWN→ city at the southern tip of Africa

MEXICO CITY→ capital city of Mexico

OTTAWA→ capital city of Canada

CAIRO→ capital city of Egypt

LAGOS→ capital city of Nigeria

LONDON→ capital city in the southern part of the United Kingdom

CHICAGO→ city in north-central United States

LOS ANGELES→ city on the west coast of the United States

HAVANA→ capital city of Cuba

SHANGHAI→ city on the east coast of China, across from Japan

HONG KONG→ city on the south coast of China, southwest of Taiwan

SUMATRA→ largest Indonesian island, near Thailand

NEW ZEALAND→ on the two large islands southeast of Australia

SYDNEY→ city on the southeast coast of Australia

MISSISSIPPI RIVER→ on the river in North America

YANGTZE RIVER→ on the river in Asia

ANDES MTNS→ on the mountain range in South America

ROCKY MTNS→ on the mountain range in North America

ALPS→ on the mountain range in Europe

WASHINGTON, D.C.→ capital city of the United States

TIERRA DEL FUEGO→ land at the southern tip of South America

PANAMA CANAL→ in Panama, connecting the Atlantic and Pacific Oceans

SUEZ CANAL→ in Egypt, connecting the Red Sea and the Mediterranean Sea

over land at the equator

in the United States near the Rocky Mountains

in the Galapagos Islands (off the coast of Ecuador)

in Zambia, southern Africa